Number Ideas Through Pictures

Number Ideas Through Pictures

By Mannis Charosh
Illustrated by Giulio Maestro

THOMAS Y. CROWELL COMPANY · NEW YORK

YOUNG MATH BOOKS

Edited by Dr. Max Beberman, Director of the Committee on
School Mathematics Projects, University of Illinois

BIGGER AND SMALLER
by Robert Froman

CIRCLES
by Mindel and Harry Sitomer

COMPUTERS
by Jane Jonas Srivastava

THE ELLIPSE
by Mannis Charosh

ESTIMATION
by Charles F. Linn

FRACTIONS ARE PARTS OF THINGS
by J. Richard Dennis

GRAPH GAMES
by Frédérique and Papy

LINES, SEGMENTS, POLYGONS
by Mindel and Harry Sitomer

LONG, SHORT, HIGH, LOW, THIN, WIDE
by James T. Fey

MATHEMATICAL GAMES FOR ONE OR TWO
by Mannis Charosh

ODDS AND EVENS
by Thomas C. O'Brien

PROBABILITY
by Charles F. Linn

RIGHT ANGLES: PAPER-FOLDING GEOMETRY
by Jo Phillips

RUBBER BANDS, BASEBALLS AND DOUGHNUTS:
A BOOK ABOUT TOPOLOGY
by Robert Froman

STRAIGHT LINES, PARALLEL LINES,
PERPENDICULAR LINES
by Mannis Charosh

WEIGHING & BALANCING
by Jane Jonas Srivastava

WHAT IS SYMMETRY?
by Mindel and Harry Sitomer

Edited by Dorothy Bloomfield, Mathematics Specialist,
Bank Street College of Education

LESS THAN NOTHING IS REALLY SOMETHING *by Robert Froman*

NUMBER IDEAS THROUGH PICTURES *by Mannis Charosh*

SPIRALS *by Mindel and Harry Sitomer*

STATISTICS *by Jane Jonas Srivastava*

VENN DIAGRAMS *by Robert Froman*

Copyright © 1974 by Mannis Charosh, Illustrations copyright © 1974 by Giulio Maestro

Library of Congress Cataloging in Publication Data   Charosh, Mannis. Number ideas through
pictures. (A Young math book)   SUMMARY: A simple introduction to numbers and their meanings.
1. Number concept—Juv. lit. [1. Number concept] I. Maestro, Giulio, illus. II. Title. QA9.C485
513'.2   73-4370

ISBN 0-690-00155-X   ISBN 0-690-00156-8 (lib. bdg.)

2 3 4 5 6 7 8 9 10

Number Ideas Through Pictures

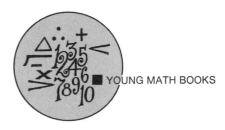

YOUNG MATH BOOKS

1, 2, 3, 4, 5, . . . These are the numbers we count with. They have many uses. But they can also be played with. Many people have found it fun to add them in different ways to form interesting patterns.

If you follow the steps in this book, you can have fun too. Try it.

You can picture numbers in many ways. You can draw small circles or dots on a piece of paper:

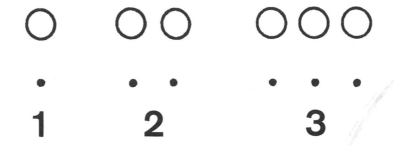

1   **2**   **3**

Or you can place on a table small objects such as:

checkers

coins

beads

or even beans.

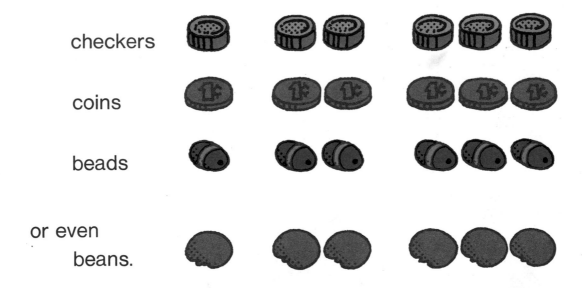

Use objects to copy each example in this book.
It will help you answer the questions.

Place 6 objects on a table:

Arrange them in pairs:

There are none left over.

Whenever we can pair a number of things off with none left over, we say that the number is EVEN. 6 is an EVEN NUMBER. Your teacher sometimes asks your class to line up by twos. If everyone has a partner, your class has an even number of children. If there is one left without a partner, we say that the number of children is ODD.

Place 5 objects on a table:

Try to arrange them in pairs:

Since there is one left over, 5 is an ODD NUMBER.

Let's picture the first ten numbers.

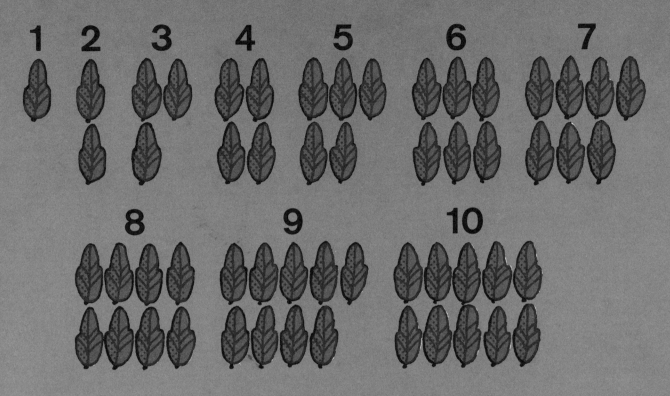

If they are written in this order, they are called CONSECUTIVE NUMBERS.

Which are the even numbers? They are 2, 4, 6, 8, 10. Do you see that the objects for these numbers are paired off? If they are written in this order, they are called CONSECUTIVE EVEN NUMBERS.

Which are the odd numbers? They are 1, 3, 5, 7, 9. Do you see that the objects for each of these numbers are paired off with one left over? If they are written in this order, they are called CONSECUTIVE ODD NUMBERS.

When you count from 1 to 10, notice the rhythm: 1 (odd), 2 (even), 3 (odd), 4 (even), 5 (odd), 6 (even), 7 (odd), 8 (even), 9 (odd), 10 (even). As you continue to count, the rhythm will stay the same.

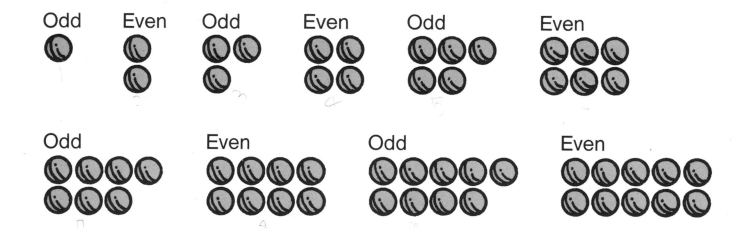

Is 17 an odd number or even number?

To find out, place 17 objects on a table. Pair them off. You should find that there is one left over. 17 is an odd number. Check your answer by saying "odd–even–odd–even . . ." as you count the objects.

Draw pictures or arrange objects for the numbers 11 to 20. Which are even? Which are odd?

Let's see what happens if we add odd and even numbers in different ways.

What kind of number do you get if you add two even numbers?

In pictures, let's add

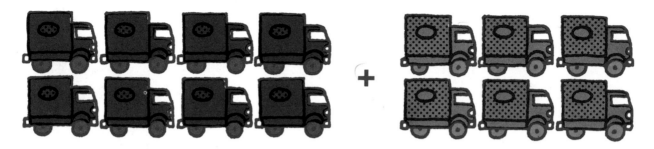

Place the two groups together like this:

You do not have to count the objects to see that they are paired off with none left over. The same thing will happen when we add any two even numbers. Do you see the rule?

EVEN NUMBER + EVEN NUMBER = EVEN NUMBER

What kind of number do you think you would get if you added two odd numbers? Would it be an odd number? An even number? Let's find out by adding these two odd numbers:

Do this with objects placed on a table.

First turn the right-hand group around like this:

Then place it next to the group at the left so that the extra objects are paired off:

You do not have to count the objects to see that they are paired off with none left over. The same thing will happen when we add any two odd numbers.

Do you see the rule?

ODD NUMBER + ODD NUMBER = EVEN NUMBER

Did you guess right?

Look at this example:

This shows that

EVEN NUMBER + ODD NUMBER = ODD NUMBER

See whether you can finish this rule:

ODD NUMBER + EVEN NUMBER = ?

We can now show without pairing that 17 is an odd number:

$$17 = 10 + 7 = \text{EVEN} + \text{ODD} = \text{ODD}$$

We can test other numbers larger than 10 in the same way. Is 14 odd or even?

$$14 = 10 + 4 = \text{EVEN} + \text{EVEN} = \text{EVEN}$$

Which of these numbers are odd? Which are even?

$$10, 11, 12, 13, 14, 15, 16, 17, 18, 19$$

Do you see that

> A TWO-DIGIT NUMBER THAT BEGINS WITH 1 IS ODD IF THE LAST DIGIT IS ODD.
> IT IS EVEN IF THE LAST DIGIT IS EVEN.

This is true even if the first digit is not 1.

Odd numbers can be pictured another way.
Here is one picture of the number 7:

To make a new kind of picture, take the upper
row of 3 objects and turn it around so that a corner
is formed like the corner of this book.

Do the same with some consecutive odd numbers:

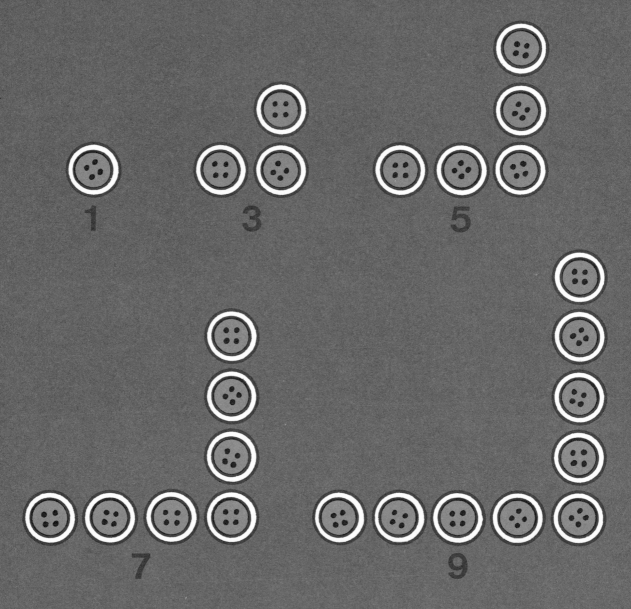

Let's see what happens when we add consecutive odd numbers, beginning with 1.

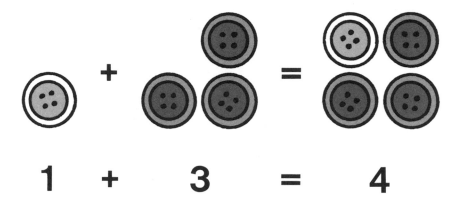

$$1 \quad + \quad 3 \quad = \quad 4$$

The shape of the final picture is a square. Therefore we call 4 a SQUARE NUMBER. Each side of the square has two objects. We say that the SQUARE of 2 is 4, or 2-SQUARED is 4.

This is a picture of a square, but it is not a picture of a square number. Pictures of square numbers always have the same number of objects in each row.

Let's add the next odd number, 5:

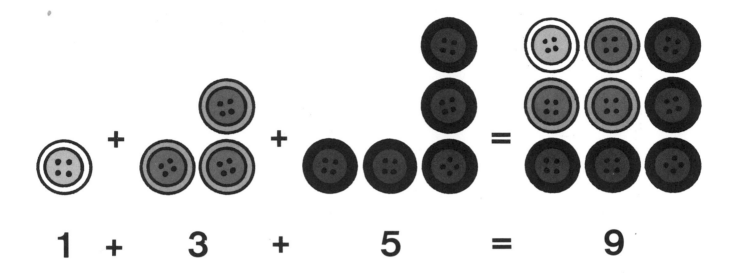

$$1 + 3 + 5 = 9$$

We get another square number. Each side of the square has 3 objects. 9 is the square of 3, or 3-squared is 9.

See what happens if you add the next odd number, 7, in the same way.

Did you get a square? What square is it? It is the square of what number? (See the next page for the answer.)

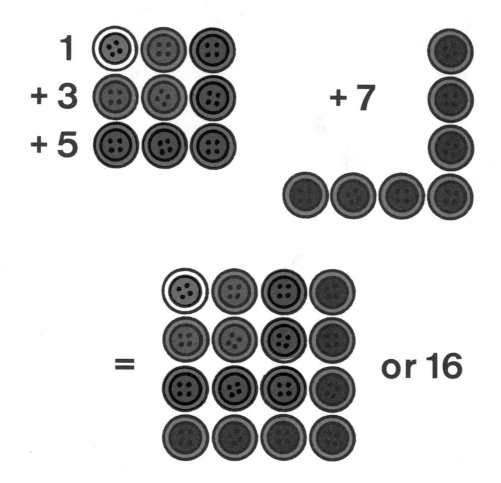

16 is a square. It is the square of 4. 4-squared is 16.

See whether you can show that the next square is 25. Also show that the next three squares after that are 36, 49, 64. If you do not have enough objects, draw circles or dots on a piece of paper.

If we think of one object as a square with one object along each side, we may say that the square of 1 is 1, or 1-squared is 1.

By adding consecutive odd numbers, beginning with 1, we built square numbers.

Let's see what happens when we add consecutive numbers, beginning with 1.

$$1 \; + \; 2 \; = \; 3$$

This picture of 3 looks like a triangle. Therefore we call 3 a TRIANGULAR NUMBER.

Let's see what happens when we add the next number:

1 + 2 + 3 = 6

6 can be pictured as a triangle, so it is a triangular number too.

1 + 2 + 3 + 4 = 10. Do you think 10 is a triangular number?

1 + 2 + 3 + 4 = 10

Only sums of consecutive numbers in a series that begins with 1 are called triangular numbers.

Show that the next triangular number is 15. Can you find other triangular numbers? The next few are: 21, 28, 36.

Just as we may think of one object as a square and consider 1 to be a square number, we may also think of one object as a triangle. 1 is a square number and a triangular number.

Did you ever see acrobats arrange themselves like the triangular number 6?

Look at tenpins which are set up for bowling.
They are arranged like the triangular number 10.

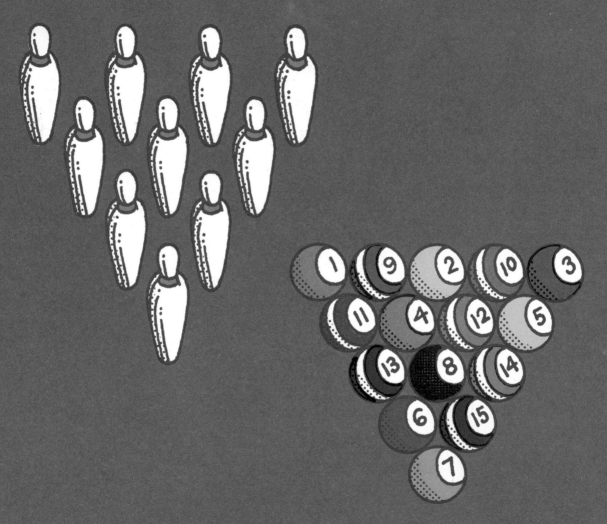

On a pool table the balls are arranged like the
triangular number 15.

These are the triangular numbers we have found: 1, 3, 6, 10, 15, 21, 28, 36. These are the square numbers we have found: 1, 4, 9, 16, 25, 36, 49, 64.

See what happens when you add two consecutive triangular numbers:

$$1 + 3 = 4$$
$$3 + 6 = 9$$
$$6 + 10 = 16$$

The sum is always a square number. With pictures it is easy to see why this must be so.

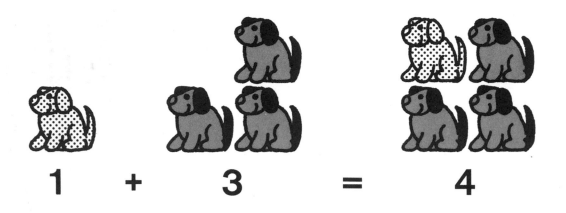

1 + 3 = 4

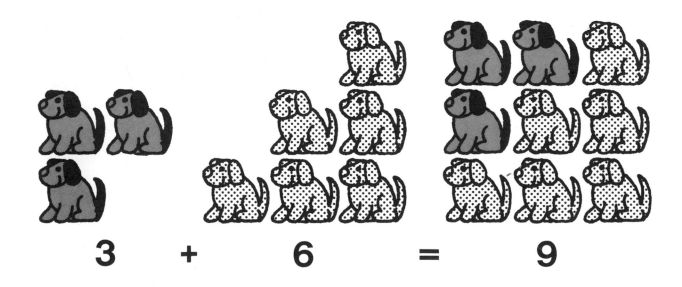

3 + 6 = 9

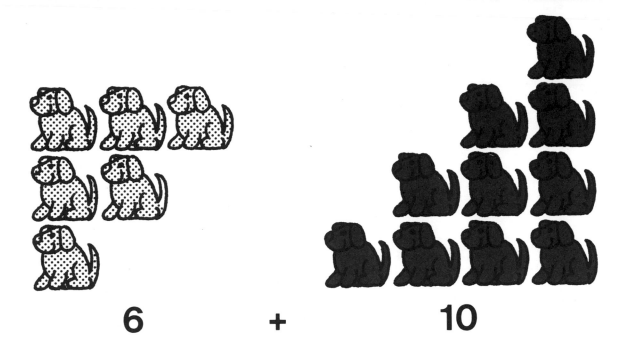

6 + 10

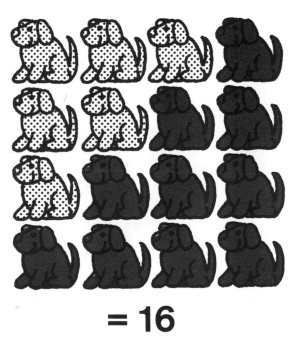

= 16

Show that the sum of 10 and the next triangular number is a square number. It will be the square of 5, or 5-squared. Build other squares by adding consecutive triangular numbers.

There are other ways of combining triangular numbers to form a square. Here is a way that someone found when playing with numbers.

Start with a triangular number such as 3:

Take it eight times and add one more object:

These can be arranged to form a square like
this:

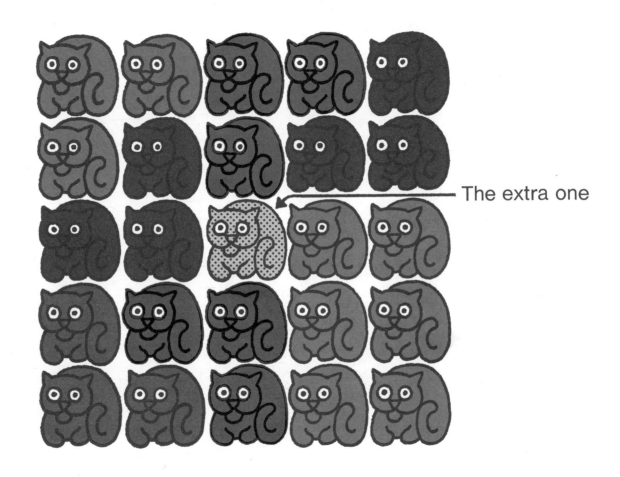

The extra one

You can form the same square in another way, using the same eight triangular numbers plus one. Mix the objects up and build a square by adding 1 + 3 + 5 and so on, until all the objects have been used. (You have done this before; see page 16.)

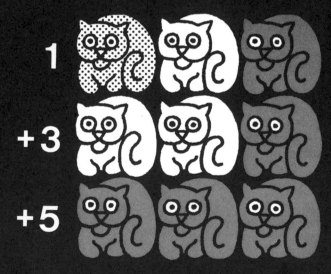

and so on...

After 3, the next triangular number is 6. See whether you can combine eight 6's and an extra one to form a square. Try to follow the same patterns as the one we just did. (The answer is on the next two pages.)

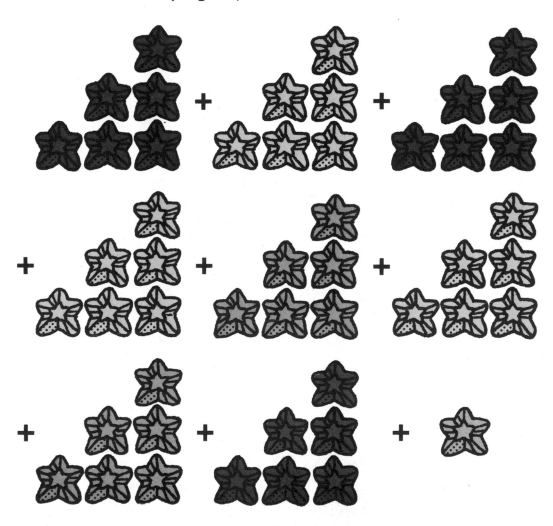

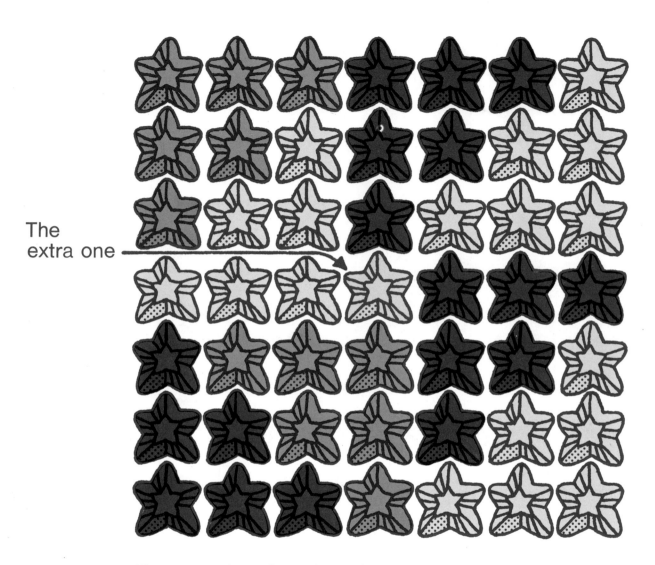

The
extra one →

If we begin with eight identical triangles plus
one we can always form a square in these two ways.
But if we begin with a square, it cannot always be
broken down into eight identical triangles plus one.

OR:

1

+3

+5

+7

+9

+11

+13

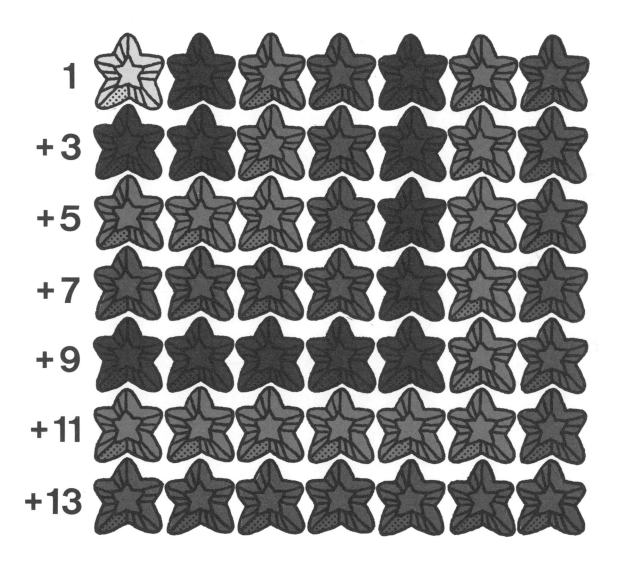

A question that has interested mathematicians is this: Can we add two squares and form a new square?

Let's try it by adding 4 and 9, or

If we try to place the objects of the smaller square around the larger square, it will look like this:

2-squared + 3-squared does not equal a square.

But 3-squared + 4-squared does equal a square:

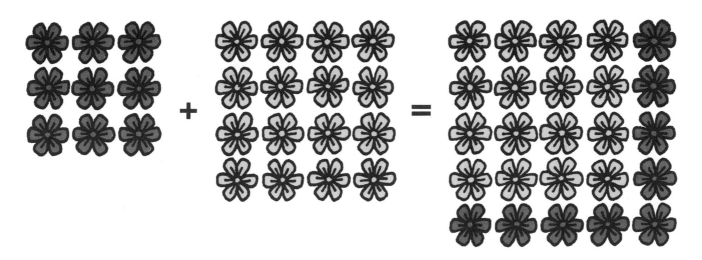

Do you see that 3-squared + 4-squared =
5-squared?

See which of the following sums of squares
will equal a square:

> 1-squared + 2-squared
> 2-squared + 4-squared
> 5-squared + 6-squared
> 6-squared + 8-squared

Only in the last case will the sum be a square. Much
more often the sum of two squares will not be a square.

If you have enough objects, try it with 5-squared + 12-squared. The sum will be 13-squared. There are many other sums of two squares which equal a square, but they are larger numbers.

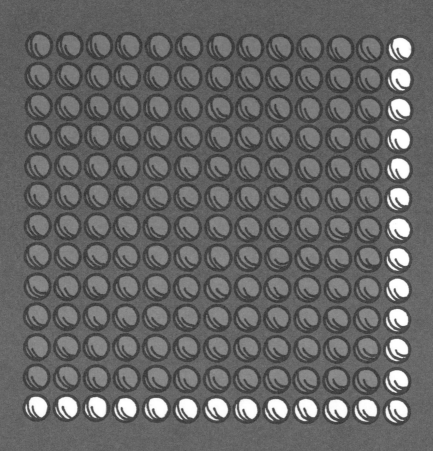

In this book you have learned about odd numbers, even numbers, square numbers, and triangular numbers. You have seen ways of combining some of these to form others. As you learn more about arithmetic, there will be many more things to learn about numbers.

This was a start.

ABOUT THE AUTHOR

Mannis Charosh has taught mathematics to high school students for many years. The author of three earlier books in Crowell's Young Math series, Mr. Charosh has also written other books, filmstrips, and motion picture narrations about mathematics and the teaching of mathematics. A chess enthusiast, Mr. Charosh is an award-winning composer of chess problems. He lives with his wife in Brooklyn, New York—where he has lived all his life.

ABOUT THE ILLUSTRATOR

Giulio Maestro was born in New York City and studied at the Cooper Union Art School and Pratt Graphics Center. Aside from picture-book illustration, he is well known for his beautiful hand lettering and his book jacket design. He enjoys etching and painting in his free time.

Mr. Maestro lives in Madison, Connecticut.